WHEN JESUS MET SANTA

WRITTEN BY
KATHLEEN M. RECHEL

ILLUSTRATED BY
JOSEPH HILS

ISBN-10: 1470077353
ISBN-13: 9781470077358

WHEN JESUS MET SANTA

WRITTEN BY
KATHLEEN M. RECHEL

ILLUSTRATED BY
JOSEPH HILS

Merry Christmas
Ashley!
Kathleen Rechel

When Jesus met Santa, He said,

"Hey big fella,

Do you mind if I drive this thing?"

"This job is for pros!"
said Santa, indignant.

"Just anyone can't
take the reins!"

"This isn't a joy ride.

You have to maneuver,

And know how to stop
a huge sleigh!"

"You have to know time zones,

And reindeer,

And forecasts,

And drive through the stars
in your way!"

"I think I can handle the route
that you're taking.
I know every inch of this place."

"I love this whole planet,
and everyone on it,
And I'd like a turn with the reins."

"I was the first Christmas...
Before there were sleigh bells.

'Twas me in the manger, you see"

"And there on the hay,
With the shepherds surrounding,
The angels were singing to me."

Then Santa's eyes were opened
And he said, "My Lord, it's You!"

"You really want to
drive the sleigh?"
And Jesus smiled, "I do!"

So they set off with the reindeer,
And the sleigh bells jingling.

And Jesus laughed when Santa cried,
"I hear the angels sing!!"

"It really is a joy ride, Lord,
With You here by my side."

"I missed this part of Christmas
When I journeyed through the night."

It's Santa and the Savior
On a sleigh ride Christmas Eve,

Spreading gifts and joy and happiness
To all who will believe!

May they come to you
this Christmas
On their joyful, merry flight,

Bringing lots of Christmas Blessings
On this Holy, Holy Night!